ISBN 978-1-5281-1893-4
PIBN 10904576

1 MONTH OF
FREE
READING

at
www.ForgottenBooks.com

By purchasing this book you are
eligible for one month membership to
ForgottenBooks.com, giving you
unlimited access to our entire
collection of over 1,000,000 titles via
our web site and mobile apps.

To claim your free month visit:

www.forgottenbooks.com/free904576

English
Français
Deutsche
Italiano
Español
Português

www.forgottenbooks.com

Mythology Photography **Fiction**
Fishing Christianity **Art** Cooking
Essays Buddhism Freemasonry
Medicine **Biology** Music **Ancient**
Egypt Evolution Carpentry Physics
Dance Geology **Mathematics** Fitness
Shakespeare **Folklore** Yoga Marketing
Confidence Immortality Biographies
Poetry **Psychology** Witchcraft
Electronics Chemistry History **Law**
Accounting **Philosophy** Anthropology
Alchemy Drama Quantum Mechanics
Atheism Sexual Health **Ancient History**
Entrepreneurship Languages Sport
Paleontology Needlework Islam
Metaphysics Investment Archaeology
Parenting Statistics Criminology
Motivational

Historic, archived document

Do not assume content reflects current
scientific knowledge, policies, or practices.

Bulbs

and

Plants

for Autumn Planting

..1902..

COX SEED CO.

411=413=415 Sansome St.,

SAN FRANCISCO, CALIFOR[N]

HARDY LILIES

The lily has long been celebrated for its rare and chaste beauty. No plants capable of being cultivated out-of-doors possess so many charms, rich and varied in color, stately and handsome in habit, profuse in variety, and of delicious fragrance. With a well selected collection, lilies may be had in bloom from June to October. They should be planted in the fall, from October 1st, as long as the ground can be worked, and in spring as soon as the frost is out of the soil until the 15th of May. The bulbs of all lilies should be planted about 6 inches deep; if they are to be sent by mail add 25 cents per dozen for postage.

Lilium Longiflorum

Auratum This magnificent variety has become one of the standard favorites of the flower garden, and is considered by many the finest of all lilies, their immense blooms measuring nearly a foot in width when fully expanded. The flowers are produced in great profusion, and are deliciously fragrant. Extra large bulbs 25c each. $2 00 per dozen; $15 00 per 100; bulbs of fine quality 15c each, $1 50 per dozen, $10 00 per 100; small bulbs, blooming size, 10c each $1 00 per dozen, $6 00 per 100

Candidum The old pure white garden lily 10c each, $1 00 per dozen; $7 00 per 100.

Harrisii Bermuda Easter Lily. A well-known beautiful white lily. Trumpet shape; very early, flowers produced in abundance and are very fragrant; 10c each. 75c per dozen; extra size, 15c each, $1 50 per dozen, $10 00 per 100

Longiflorum A well-known, beautiful snow white lily, very fragrant; 10c each, $1 00 per dozen, $6 00 per 100

Pardalinum Scarlet, shading to rich yellow, freely spotted purple brown; 25c each. $2 50 per dozen

Speciosum Album Pure white and very fragrant. Extra large bulbs 15c each, $1 50 per dozen; $10 00 per 100; medium size, 10c each, $1 00 per dozen, $8 00 per 100.

Speciosum, Roseum, or Rubrum

Rose, spotted with crimson, extra large bulbs, 3 each, $1 50 per dozen, $10 00 per 100.

Tigrinum (*Tiger Lily*) Single, orange, salmon, spotted black; 10c each, 75c per dozen.

Tigrinum Flore Pleno

The double tiger lily. A splendid sort; 15c each; $1 50 per dozen.

Washingtonianum One of the most beautiful lilies of California; flowers erect, pure white, with bright scarlet spots; they are produced in great numbers, and very fragrant; plant one foot deep in well drained soil; 25c each; $2 50 per dozen.

LILY OF THE VALLEY

Ready in November. This beautiful, dainty little flower needs no introduction. All plant lovers have already made its acquaintance. Its favorite spot in the garden is in some cool, shady place, in deep, rich soil—not too heavy. The roots should be set about six inches apart and about two inches deep. Plants or Pips, as they are called, are especially prepared for pot culture. They should be potted in good, rich

Lilium Auratum

soil, placing five or six of them in a four-inch pot, and covering them with about an inch of the soil; set the pots away in some cool place in the dark to get the pips well rooted, when they may be removed to the warmth of the green house or living room. Keep them well watered: in a few weeks the flowers will shoot out.

Fine pips, per doz. 25c; post paid per 100, $1.50.

Our beautifully illustrated Annual Catalogue issued January 1st, will be sent free by mail on application.

BULBS, TREES, PLANTS, &c., &c.

HYACINTHS

Hardly need special praise, as every one knows them to be among the most useful and popular of hardy bulbs. It is not only a general favorite for the garden, but is exceedingly popular as a window flower, from the facility with which it may be forced into bloom either in pots or glasses, which will make the window or conservatory beautiful during the dull, cheerless months of winter.

Five-inch pots are best for single bulbs, rich soil mixed with a little sand, three to four in an eight-inch pot will make a good show. Out doors any garden soil will answer. Plant four to six inches deep.

HYACINTHS—Single Varieties

Light Blue, 50c per doz.; $4 00 per 100
Red and Rose, 50c per doz.; $4.00 per 100
Rose, 50c per doz; $4.00 per 100
White and Blush, 50c per doz.; $4.00 per 100.
Pure White, 50c per doz ; $4 00 per 100
Yellow, 50c per doz., $4.00 per 100.
All Colors, mixed, 50c per doz.; $4.00 per 100

HYACINTHS—Double Varieties

Blue, all shades, 60c per doz ; $4.50 per 100
Light Blue, 60c per doz.; $4.50 per 100
Red, 60c per doz.; $4.50 per 100
Rose, 60c per doz.; $4.50 per 100
Dark Blue, 60c per doz.; $4.50 per 100
Dark Rose, 60c per doz ; $4.50 per 100
Pure White, 60c per doz.; $4.50 per 100
Yellow, 60c per doz.; $4.50 per 100...
All Colors, 60c per doz.; $4.50 per 100.

NAMED DUTCH HYACINTHS—All Extra Size Bulbs

15c each; $1.25 per doz.

Rose Gem, single rose
Robert Steiger, single; fine deep crimson, large truss
Norma, single; blush pink, large bells; early
Gertrude, single; rosy pink; splendid for pots
Splendens, single; white
Granduer a Merveille, single; blush white; large truss
Baron von Tuyl, single; violet blue, large truss; early
Grand Lilas, single; light blue
Grand Maitre, single; large spike, porcelain blue
King of Blues, single; dark blue
Princess Royal, double; red purple center; good truss
Bouquet Royal, pure white; very double
La Virginite, double; pale blush; very early
Grootvorst, double; rosy blush; fine truss
Czar Nicholas, double, light pink; early
General Antink, double, light blue
Blocksburg, double; lavender marbled; fine truss
Flevo, double; pure white; fine truss
Bride of Haarlem, large double; white

ROMAN HYACINTHS

This beautiful and very valuable variety, if planted in September and gently forced, will bloom in November, or flowering may be retarded until Christmas by keeping in a cool place. The flowers, which are smaller than those of the ordinary hyacinth, are produced in great profusion, each bulb throwing up three or four spikes of delicately scented, clear white blossoms, highly recommended for parlor decorations.

White Romans—Extra quality bulbs, per doz., 50c; per 100 $3.50

TULIPS

Tulips are such universal favorites that it is not necessary to expiate upon their merits here. Being perfectly hardy, their ease of culture combined with beauty of form and gorgeous coloring, render them the most popular bulb grown for spring bedding, as well as for winter flowering in the greenhouse and window garden. Culture, the same as the hyacinth.

SINGLE AND DOUBLE TULIPS IN MIXTURE

These are especially recommended for bedding in large or small masses, where economy in expenditure as well as brilliancy in effect is desired. Our mixtures are made up of bright-colored varieties.

Please state whether you wish single, double or both.

All Colors—Fine mixed; superior to ordinary Mixed Tulips; as sent out, per doz., 25c; per 100, $1.50

NAMED SINGLE EARLY TULIPS

Artus—Dwarf, bright red; fine bold flowers; 25c per doz., $1.50 per 100.
Chrysolora—Pure golden yellow, per doz., 30c; per 100, $2.00
Couleur Cardinal—Brilliant crimson; splendid for bedding; per doz., 50c; per 100, $3.50

TULIPS, SINGLE—Continued

Crimson King (Roi Cramoise)—Fine showy bedder; large flowers, bright crimson, per doz., 30c; per 100, $2.00

Duchesse de Parma—Orange red banded yellow; very large fine flower; 25c per doz.; $1.50 per 100

Duc Van Tholl, Scarlet—Intense dazzling scarlet. Very desirable for early forcing; per doz., 35c; $2.25 per 100

Duc Van Tholl. Rose Colored—Desirable for bedding; per doz., 35c; $2.75 per 100

Duc Van Tholl. Yellow—40c per doz.; $3.00 per 100

Duc Van Tholl, White—40c per doz.; $3.00 per 100

Joost Van Vordel—Deep cherry red, with white feather through center of petals. 30c doz. $2.00 per 100

Keiserskroon (Grand Duc)—Red, bordered golden yellow. Extra large flower. One of the very finest tulips for forcing or bedding; per doz., 30c; $2.00 per 100.

La Reine (Queen Victoria)—White, slightly shaded pink. A favorite forcing variety, extra fine for bedding; per doz., 25c; $1.50 per 100

Pottebaker, Yellow—Yellow, with light scarlet stripe, per doz., 35c; $2.00 per 100

Parrot Tulips

Pottebaker, Yellow—35c per doz.; $2.00 per 100

Pottebaker, White—Finest white forcing tulip. Extra large flower. Very early. Also extra fine for bedding; per doz., 35c; $2.25 per 100

Pottebaker, Scarlet (Verboom)—Very fine bright scarlet. Excellent for forcing or bedding; per doz., 35c; $2.25 per 100

Rosamundi Huykman—Rose pink with broad white stripes in the flower, fine stem. Extra fine bedder; per doz., 35c

Rose Grisdelin—Lovely delicate pink. Best pink for early forcing; also fine for bedding; per doz., 35c; $2.50 per 100

Vander Neer—Rich claret purple; very fine flower; 35c per doz.; $2.25 per 100

Vermillion Brilliante—Dazzling vermillion, magnificent, fine for pots and massing; per doz., 50c

Yellow Prince—The standard yellow forcing tulip; also fine for bedding. Shows orange tint when bedded; per doz., 35c; $2.25 per 100.

NAMED DOUBLE TULIPS

These are the earliest blooming tulips, and are greatly prized for pot culture during winter. In the garden they bloom with the crocus, and are welcome heralders of spring. Do not omit this charming class.

Double Late Tulips—Mixed; per doz., 30c.; $1.75 per 100

Duke of York—Very double carmine rose; edged white and suffused rose; per doz. 25c; $1.75 per 100.

Imperator Rubrorum—Splendid bright scarlet, yellow base, a fine full double; 35c per doz.; $2.25 per 100

La Candeur—Pure white. Fine for bedding and also for Easter forcing; per doz., 35; $2.25 per 100.

Rex Rubrorum—Extra fine scarlet for bedding. Large, full and double flower; doz., 35c. $2.25 per 100

Rosine—Blush white, tinged rose; per doz. 30c; $2 00 per 100

Tournesol—Showy tulip, orange scarlet, with broad yellow tips and yellow base; 35c per doz.; $2.25 per 100.

Tournesol Yellow—35c per doz.; $2.25 per 100

All Colors in fine mixture—Per doz., 25c; $1.50 per 100

Single Tulips

BYBLŒMEN TULIPS

Late or May-flowering Garden Tulips, blotched, striped or feathered with blue, lilac, violet, purple; or black on white ground; 35c per doz; $2.25 per 100

BIZARRE TULIPS

Late or May-flowering Garden Tulips, grand rich flowers of perfect shape, having yellow ground color, feathered or striped with crimson, purple or white; 35c per doz.; $2.25 per 100.

PARROT TULIPS

These belong to the May-flowering tulips, and have immense attractive flowers of singular and picturesque forms, and brilliant and varied colors. The petals are curiously fringed or cut and the form of the flower, especially before it opens, resembles the neck of a parrot. They are of endless variety of form and color, and should be grown in every flower garden in quantities. Fine mixed, per doz., 50c; $3.00 per 100

DARWIN TULIPS

Darwin Tulips belong to the late flowering section, are destined to be extensively grown for bedding or massing purposes. The flowers are very large, of symmetrical form, and are borne on *tall, strong stems, often two feet high.* They surpass in colors and brilliancy anything before known in tulips. The colors are so glowing and bright that in the sunlight the effect is fairly dazzling. They include almost every conceivable color and shades from the daintiest blue to the darkest violet, from the soft rose to the most brilliant red, and from light brown to what is believed to be the darkest black in the floral world. Mixed colors, per doz., 50c; $3.50 per 100.

Black Calla

CROCUS

The Crocus is one of the first flowers of spring, and one of the best for blooming in the house during winter. Half a dozen bulbs may be planted in a pot, and will make a very pretty show. For garden culture plant bulbs two inches deep and two inches apart. They are so cheap and pretty they ought to be found in every garden.

Large Yellow—Per doz., 15c; per 100, 50c
Blue—Per doz., 10c; per 100, 50c
White—Per doz., 10c; per 100, 50c
Striped—Per doz., 10c; per 100, 50c
Fine Mixed—Per doz., 10c; per 100, 40c
Mammoth Yellow—Per doz, 20c., per 100, 75c

CHINESE SACRED LILY

This variety is the Tazetta, or bunch flowering Narcissus, and is the sort grown extensively by the Chinese for use in their New Year festivals. The bulbs we offer are very large, averaging three to four inches in diameter, and they throw up several stems when well grown, the flowers are produced in profusion. Flowers are pure white with a lemon or orange cup. The Chinese method is as follows: Fill a bowl, or some similar vessel, with pebbles, in which place the bulb, setting it about one-half its depth, so that it will be held firmly, then fill with water to the top of the pebbles and place in a warm sunny window. The bulb will at once commence a rapid growth and bloom in two or three weeks. Bulbs are hardy, and bloom well in open ground. Each, 15c; per doz., $1.50.

NARCISSUS OR DAFFODILS

The wonderful new varieties have awakened an interest and enthusiasm among the lovers of flowers that has placed this, "the flower of the poets," in the front rank of popularity. They turn our gardens, lawns and woodland walks into gorgeous masses of gold and silver, with a fragrance that is enchanting. They are equally valuable for growing in pots for winter, flowering in the house with the hyacinth, and should be cultivated in the same way, three roots at least in a four or five inch pot. The cut flowers of daffodils are much in demand for bouquets and vases.

SINGLE NARCISSUS
(Daffodils)

Bicolor Horsefieldi—Large; golden yellow trumpet. Each, 10c; per doz., 75c

Golden Spur—Enormous; deep yellow trumpet Each, 10c; per doz., 85c

Incomparable—Single; yellow. Each, 5c; per doz , 50c

Princeps—Single; early; yellow trumpet. Each, 5c; per doz., 25c; $1.50 per 100.

Trumpet Major—Golden yellow, finest for winter blooming. Each, 5c; per doz., 35c

Poeticus Ornatus—Early for forcing, the finest; Each, 5c; per doz , 25c

Sir Watkin (*Incomparable Giganteus*—A grand golden flower. Each, 15c; per doz , $1.00

Stella—Yellow cup, white perianthe. Each, 5c per doz., 50c

Empress—Broad rich yellow trumpet, with sulphur tinge. Its foliage is very strong and the blooms enormous in size. Probably the most superb Narcissus in cultivation. Flowers of good substance. Each, 10c; per doz., 85c

Mixed—Single sorts. Per doz., 20c; $1.25 per 100

DOUBLE NARCISSUS
(Daffodils)

Von Sion—The finest of all double yellow daffodils, used extensively for forcing as well as for bedding outdoors. Per doz., 30c; per 100, $2.00

Mixed—Double. Each 5c; per doz., 40c

JONQUILS

Much prized for their charming golden and deliciously sweet-scented flowers, perfectly hardy, and flowering very early in the spring, also admirably adapted for winter flowering in the house; three to six bulbs in a four or five inch pot.

Single—Sweet scented; yellow. Per doz., 10c; 75c per 100

Double—Sweet scented; yellow. Per doz., 40c; $2.50 per 100

Campernelle—Large, six-lobed yellow flowered, jonquil, four to six on a stem; fine. Per doz., 15c; $1.00 per 100

BEGONIAS

Tuberous Rooted — Ready for delivery in November.

The wonderful beauty of this class of Begonias, and its adaptability to almost all situations, has made it a general favorite for both pot culture and summer garden decoration. They are now being used by thousands for bedding purposes. We offer the following distinct varieties:—

Single Varieties—White, scarlet, rose, yellow, dark, blood-red or orange. Each, 10c; per doz., $1.00

Double Varieties—Red, white, rose or yellow. Each, 15c; per doz., $1.50.

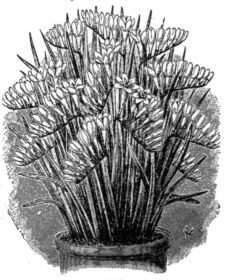

Freesia

AMARYLLIS

Belladona Major—This splendid species is perfectly hardy with lovely pink and white flowers. Plant the bulb six to eight inches deep in sand with good fibrous loam pressed around it, and do not disturb for years. After they become established they will give grand masses of bloom. Each, strong, 35c; 20c for smaller bulbs.

Johnsonii—A very popular variety, wine-red, with a white stripe down each petal; an early and abundant bloomer; a specially robust grower. Each, 50c

CRINUM AMERICANUM

Large spikes of beautiful white, sweet-scented flowers. Each, 30c

DIELYTRA SPECTABILIS

Bleeding Heart — Though not so common, bears long, graceful chains of pendulous heart-shaped pink flowers of exquisite beauty; fine for winter blooming. Each, 25c (Ready December)

ANEMONES

Highly ornamental spring and summer flowering plants, having both single and double flowers, the colors of which are wonderfully beautiful, running through all shades of blue, scarlet, rose, white, lavender, etc.

Single Superfine—All colors, mixed. Per doz., 15c per 100, $1.00

Brilliant Scarlet—Per doz., 25c; per 100, $1.00

Blue—Per doz., 25c; Per 100, $1 50

The Bride—Pure white, large flower. Per doz., 30c; per 100, $1.75

Double—In extra fine mixture. Per doz., 20c; $1.50 per 100

ANEMONE FULGENS

Grand variety for winter flowers; splendid forcing variety. The rich dazzling scarlet flowers and light elegant growth render it most attractive. It is invaluable for cutting, as it lasts a long time in water. Admirable for selling in bunches. Per doz., 50c; $3.00 per 100

RANUNCULUS

Among dwarf flowers these are unrivalled for lovely form and bright and attractive colors. They flower profusely in pots in the house.

Double Persian—Mixed colors. Per doz., 25c; $1.50 per 100

Double French—Mixed colors. Per doz., 25c; $1.50 per 100

Turban—Mixed colors. Per doz., 25c; $1.50 per 100

SCILLA SIBERICA, OR SQUILL
(Star Hyacinth)

Scilla Siberica is one of the loveliest spring flowers. If planted in pots and kept indoors it may be had in bloom as early as Christmas. Beautiful porcelain blue flowers. Per doz., 15c; 75c per 100.

IXIAS

The Ixia is a beautiful little winter flowering bulb, with low, slender, graceful spikes of bloom. They present almost every known color, three or four different hues appearing in almost every flower. Per doz., 15c; $1.00 per 100

Iris Kæmpferi

FREESIA

Refracta Alba—This is one of the most popular and charming bulbs for pot culture, flowering in the winter and spring in the conservatory or window garden. Six or eight bulbs should be planted in a four-inch pot. They force readily, and can be had in bloom by Christmas, if desired. The flowers are produced six to eight on a stem; are particularly useful for cutting. The flowers are pure white, with a yellow blotched throat, and are exquisitely fragrant. Extra large bulbs, per doz., 15c; per 100, $1.00.

SPARAXIS

Exceedingly large and beautiful; blooms about two inches across; of the most telling combinations and of the brightest shades of color. Mixture of the finest sorts. Per doz., 15c; $1.00 per 100

SNOWDROPS

These are the first flowers to greet us in spring, their pretty, drooping, snow-white blossoms appearing in March, a few days ahead of Scilla Siberica, to which they form a charming contrast. They are also splendid for house culture in pots, blooming usually at Christmas.

Single White—Per doz., 15c; 75c per 100
Double White—Per doz., 30c; $2.00 per 100

TUBEROSES

Dwarf Pearl—Its value over the common variety consists in its flower being nearly double in size, imbricated like a rose, growing only eighteen inches to two feet. Per doz., 40c. (Ready December)

CALLAS

Calla (*Lily of the Nile*)—An elegant and popular plant. Extra large plants, 10c; per doz.. $1 00
Calla, Black—Immense, velvety-purple, sweet-scented flowers. Selected bulbs Each, 10c; doz.$1.00
Calla, Spotted Leaf—Very Ornamental; dark green leaves, spotted with white. Each, 10c; per doz., $1.00

CYCLAMEN

These are among the most beautiful and interesting winter and spring flowering bulbs for the window. Not only are the flowers of striking beauty, but the foliage is also highly ornamental. There are no plants better adapted for pot culture, and few that produce such a profusion of bloom; the flowers range through many shades, pink, crimson, white, some being beautifully spotted; delicately fragrant.
Assorted Colors—Each, 15c; per doz., $1.50

GLOXINIA

One of the choicest bulbs for pot and house culture. Beautiful trumpet-shaped flowers, violet, rose, and blue crimson. Mixed, 25c each.

TIGRIDIAS

Peacock Flower or Mexican Shell Flower
Extremely handsome summer flowering bulbs, growing about two feet high, producing large gorgeous flowers, exquisitely spotted. They flower very freely throughout the summer, particularly if the bulbs are planted in a warm, sunny position. Ready in November.
Conchiflora—Dark yellow, large red spots. Each, 5c; per doz., 30c
Pavonia Grandiflora—Very large, bright crimson, center mottled with yellow. Each, 5c; doz 50c.
Grandiflora Alba—Large ivory white, spotted at the base with red on a yellowish background. Each, 10c; per doz., 75c

IRIS KÆMPFERI

The newest varieties of this King of Iris, recently introduced from Japan, are marvels of beauty and stateliness. Think of a plant sending up to a height of three feet a dozen flower spikes, each spike bearing from two to four enormous blossoms eight or ten inches across and of the most delicate and beautiful colors, markings and combinations, white, indigo, violet, lavender, mauve, sky-blue, royal purple, blush, yellow. When you see them you will realize they are infinitely more grand and beautiful than your imagination could portray. Each, 20c; 3 for 50c

SPANISH IRIS

For garden or pot culture the Spanish Irises are a beautiful and easily grown flower. Those who plant them will find that they are very beautiful indeed.
Mixed Colors—20c per doz., $1.25 per 100
Blue Flag—Deep purple; 25c doz., $1.50 per 100
La Tendresse—Pure white, large flower; strong tall stem; 25c per doz.; $1.50 per 100
Louise—Light blue; fine for cutting; 25c per doz.; $1.50 per 100
Plet Hein—Olive brown, shaded blue; 25c per doz.; $1.50 per 100
William First—The best yellow; large flower. Each 5c. per doz., 40c

AGAPANTHUS

(The Blue African Lily)
Umbellatus—The old favorite; flowers bright blue. These are noble ornaments on lawns, in pots, or tubs or for the decoration of the greenhouse. Foliage luxuriant and graceful, flowers borne in clusters of 20 to 30, and measure fully a foot across. The flower stalks frequently attain a height of three feet—the flowers opening in succession for a long period during the summer and autumn. 25c each; $2.50 per doz.

MONTBRETIAS

6 for 25c; 45c per doz.

Gladioli

GLADIOLI

Named varieties, each 10c.; per doz. $1.00, except where noted

Addison—Dark amaranth, with white stripes.

African—Darkest crimson black, with a pure white blotch in the throat. The darkest and one of the finest colors; large flower and spike.

Ajax—Beautiful striped.

Angelene—White, showy and effective.

Amalthee—Pure white, with violet-red blotch, ground of the corolla velvety-velvet, the lower petals slightly tinted with lilac.

Archduchess Marie-Christine — White, slightly tinted with lilac, flamed rosy-carmine.

Cameleon—Compound truss of large slaty-lilac flowers flamed orange, with white bands down the middle of each petal; large, creamy-white blotch, streaked violet. Each, 15c; per doz., $1.50

Duchess of Edinburgh—An eminent English culturist describes the variety as follows: "A flower of fine form and great substance; a plant of strong growth, attaining a height of six feet. Purplish rose, with a carmine stripe on the lower divisions; without exception the finest variety ever sent out."

Martha Washington—Light yellow, of large size, in a well-arranged spike; lower petals tinged with rose.

Mlle. Maries Mies—Delicate rose, flamed with carmine; slight blotch of rosy purple, dense spike.

Penelope—Blush white; lower petals tinted yellow, streaked carmine.

Richard Cœur de Lion—Fine spike of large flowers of a bright crimson-red color flamed and edged with garnet; lower petals spotted and blotched golden yellow. Each, 15c; per doz. $1.50

Snow White—All that need be said about this grand novelty is that it is absolutely *pure snow white*, the only pure white Gladiolus in existence. It also has large, well-open flowers, and an enormous spike of the most perfect and beautiful shape. Each, 15c; per doz., $1.50

The Bride (*Colvilli Alba*) Beautiful; purest white flowers, set closely on stem; most valuable for forcing for cut flowers. 3 for 10c, 30c per doz.; $1.75 per 100

Grand Mixed Gladiolus—Per doz., 75c; per 100, $5.00

JAPANESE TREE PÆONIES

The finest of Pæonies. Like most Japanese importations, quite hardy, and remarkable for their great perfection of flowers, both in size and richness of color. They grow to the size of a large shrub, increasing in vigor and size of flowers season after season. Choice imported varieties. Each, $1.00.

PÆONIES—Hardy Herbaceous

Herbaceous Pæonies are among the showiest and most useful plants and are becoming popular with the public. They are hardy and admirably adapted to our climate, growing well in almost any situation or soil, although the flowers will be finer and the color brighter if planted in a deep, rich loam, well-manured. We offer a splendid assortment in twelve distinct varieties. Price, each, 30c; per doz., $3.00

ABBREVIATED PLANT LIST

For Complete List, Send for our Beautifully Illustrated
Annual Catalogue, issued January 1st. FREE.

HARDY EVERGREEN TREES AND SHRUBS.

Acacia dealbata (*Silver Wattle*).
—Very free flowering, in panicles, of deep
lemon color; 2 to 3 feet. 25c each.

Acacia decurrens—(*Black Wattle*)—An elegant tree, with beautiful
feathery foliage; 2 to 3 feet; 25c each.

Acacia latifolia—Resembles the
following variety, but the leaves are longer
and the tree more floriferous; 4 to 5 feet;
35c each.

Acacia melanoxylon (*Black
Wood Tree*)—A strong, upright-growing
tree. 10c, 15c and 35c each.

Acacia mollissima—A fine. erect-
growing tree, with glaucous, green feathery foliage. Flowers yellow, and borne
in racemes; 2 to 3 feet; 25c each.

Araucaria Bidwellii—A magnificent tree. Branches in regular whorls.
Closely set with spiny, shining. deep-
green leaves. Very handsome for the
lawn, and by far the finest and most attractive of all evergreen trees. 75c and
$1.50 each.

Araucaria Excelsa (*Norfolk
Island Pine*)—One of the handsomest of
all trees. Pyramidal in form, and very
symmetrical. Hardy only in protected
locations. Excellent for parlor decoration. 50c, 75c, $1.00, $1.50 and $2.00 each,
according to size.

Araucaria Imbricata (*Chili Pine
or Monkey Tree*)—A fine tree, of regular
pyramidal form. Leaves dark green,
broad, thick, pointed and overlapping
each other. 50c, 75c, $1.00, $1.50, $2.00,
and $2.50 each.

Aucuba Japonica (*Gold Dust
Tree*)— Handsome, hardy evergreen
shrubs, with large. bright, green leaves,
beautifully marked yellow. They make
splendid conservatory or parlor plants.
When planted out of doors they should be set in a half shady loca-
tion. Each, 35c

Araucaria Bidwellii   Photographed by Cox Seed Co.

Azalea Indica—The flowers of these are of
unsurpassed beauty, borne in large clusters above the
small leaves. Blooms from January to April. Colors
very rich. Should be planted in a shady, moist loca-
tion. 75c and $1.00 each.

Bamboo falcata—A very ornamental species,
attaining a height of twenty feet. 60c each.

Bamboo Kumasasa—Small, slender, grassy
foliage. 50c each.

Bamboo Mitis—One of the largest bamboos. It
grows to a height of twenty-eight to thirty-eight feet.
The canes are used extensively for furniture work,
water pipes, etc. 75c each.

Bamboo Black—This variety attains a height
of thirty feet. The canes are black. Used for making
walking sticks, umbrellas handles, etc. 50c. each.

Bamboo, Quiloi—A very large growing sort.
Attaining a height of forty feet.

Berberis Darwinii—This is the finest of berberis. Flowers orange yellow, and deliciously fragrant. 50c each

Broom, Scotch, Yellow (*Genista*)—A very
handsome shrub. with drooping branches and covered
in the spring with bright yellow pea-shaped flowers.
Very effective for grouping. Two to three feet. 40c
each.

Broom, Scotch, White—Two to three feet.
40c each.

Broom, Spanish—An upright-growing shrub.
Flowers yellow, produced very freely in the spring and
summer, on long, pendulous, round, leafless branches.
Three feet. 60c each.

Bursaria spinosa—The foliage of this strik-
ingly handsome evergreen is small and heathlike.
The flowers are small, pure white. appearing in great
profusion. One and a half feet, 35c each.

EVERGREEN TREES AND SHRUBS—Continued.

Bamboo.   Photographed by Cox Seed Co.

Camellias—Are acknowledged to be the finest winter-flowering shrubs in cultivation. They will grow freely in any fair garden soil, and require but little attention after the first year. DOUBLE RED, WHITE AND PINK—75c and $1.00 each.

Camphor Tree (*Laurus camphora*)—A fast-growing, very symmetrical, ornamental tree, thriving in the very poorest soil. Bright green foliage; well adapted for a lawn. 60c each.

Cistus (*Rock Rose*)—Elegant shrub, having terminal flower stalks bearing one or more pink flowers, resembling those of the Dog Rose. 25c each.

Cypress Monterey—A native of California, and one of the most desirable of evergreens. Very extensively planted for hedges. Transplanted in boxes. 100, $2.50; per 1,000, $20.00; pot grown, one to one and a half feet high, 15c each; $1.25 per 10.

Daphne. Pink Flowering—One and a half feet. $1.00 each.

Daphne. White Flowering—A low growing shrub, with dark, bright green foliage, and very fragrant white flowers. One and a half feet. Each $1.00.

Diosma Alba (*Breath of Heaven*)—A handsome little shrub, with heathlike foliage, and small, white, star-shaped flowers. The leaves when bruised, emit a sweet perfume. 35c each; $3.00 per 10; large plants, 50c each.

Eucalyptus citriodora—A unique variety. Leaves highly perfumed like the Lemon Verbena. 25c and 35c each.

Eucalyptus corynocalyx (*Sugar Gum*)— Pot grown, three feet, 30c each

Eucalyptus globulus (*Tasmanian Blue Gum*)— Pot grown, two to three feet, 15c each; $1.00 per 10; transplanted in boxes, $2.50 per 100; $20 per 1,000

Eucalyptus leucoxylon (*Crimson-flowered Eucalyptus*)—A very ornamental species, having large and beautiful flowers. Blooms when quite small. Pot grown, one and one-half feet, 25c each

Eucalyptus viminalis—Recommended as hardy and suitable for exposed situations. Pot grown, one and a half feet, 15c each; $1.00 per 10

Eucalyptus robusta (*Swamp Mahogany*)—Thrives best in low-lying locations, especially near the coast. Pot grown, one and one-half feet, 15c each; three to four feet, 30c each; $2.50 per 10

Eucalyptus rostrata (*Red Gum*)—Well known and highly esteemed. Pot grown, one and one-half feet. 15c each.

Eugenia Australis (*Rose Apple*)—Handsome shrub, grown in the East Indies for its fruit. The flowers are pure white and borne in great profusion. One and one-half feet, 35c each.

Euonymus (Duc d'Anjou)—A beautiful shrub, the center of the leaves being variegated with a golden yellow. One foot, 35c each.

Escalonia rubra—Rather a pretty shrub, producing immense quantities of small red flowers. Does well in windy and exposed locations. One foot, 25c each.

Fabiana imbricata—A very pretty heath-like shrub of erect growth, producing pure white tube-shaped flowers in great profusion. When in bloom it is a most lovely shrub. 15c each.

Grevillea robusta (*Australian Silk Oak*)—A splendid fern-leaved evergreen tree, which makes a magnificent pot plant for all sorts of decorative purposes. Flowers, golden yellow. Planted out in this State it soon forms a magnificent lawn or shade tree. Price of fine pot-grown plants, 10c, 25c and 50c each.

Habrothamnus elegans—A strong-growing shrub, bearing panicles of small trumpet-shaped, purplish red flowers. Makes a grand effect on a lawn or trained against a wall or porch. 20c each.

Heath (White)—A handsome, compact-growing shrub, with light feathery foliage. The flowers are white, completely covering the bush in May and June, Pot grown, one and a half feet, 35c each.

Holly, European—A small tree, with shining, dark green, thorny leaves, somewhat resembling the oak in form. In winter the tree is covered with bright red berries. Boxed, two and a half feet, $2.00 each.

Juniper, Irish—Short, sea-green foliage. A distinct and beautiful variety of conical outline, upright and dense growth. Boxed, four feet, $2.00 each.

Laurel, English—A fine, large evergreen, with broad, shining green leaves. Produces large panicles of creamy-white flowers, followed by purple berries. One foot, 25c

Laurel, Portugal—A compact, pyramidal small tree (or large shrub), with glossy, dark green leaves. The flowers come in large panicles of creamy white, and are fragrant. 35c each.

EVERGREEN TREES AND SHRUBS—Continued.

Laurustinus—A well-known winter-flowering shrub, of great beauty, producing an abundance of white flowers. One foot, 25c each, $2.00 per 10.

Ligustrum Japonicum (Japan Privet) Produces large clusters of white flowers. Slightly fragrant, followed by purplish blue berries. Leaves glossy, leathery, dark green. A large-growing shrub (or small tree). Balled, two to three feet, 35c each; $2.50 per 10.

Loquat, Giant—This tree produces a very delicious fruit. A handsome shrub. 25c and 35c each.

Magnolia, Grandiflora—The most noble of American evergreen trees. Foliage is thick, brilliant green in the upper surface and rusty underneath. The flowers are pure white, of immense size, and very fragrant. Price, pot grown, two to three feet, 75c each.

Magnolia Grandiflora Exoniensis —A lovely evergreen species, with large leathery, bright green leaves, that look as if made of wax, a foot or eighteen inches long and four inches wide. In addition to the beauty of the foliage, it bears large, fragrant white flowers. Strong, pot-grown plants, three feet, $1.00.

Melaleuca Styphilodes—Upright growing shrub, with fine, feathery, plume-like foliage. Two feet, 35c each.

New Zealand Flax Variegated — This is an extremely ornamental plant. The leaves are sword-like in appearance, beautifully edged with silver. Strong clumps, 75c each.

Pepper Tree—A most popular shade and ornamental tree, with fine, feathery foliage. Producing clusters of reddish berries in autumn. 25c, 35c and 50c each.

Pine, Monterey (*Insignis*)—The most desirable pine for shade, and more extensively planted than any other variety in this State. Transplanted in boxes, $4.00 per 100; pot grown, two feet, 10c each; 75c per 10; balled, two to three feet, 25c each.

Pittosporum eugenoides—A very handsome upright growing shrub, with silvery light green leaves and black stems. A good hedge plant and very ornamental as an individual. Pot-grown, one foot, 20c each; $1.50 per 10.

Pittosporum nigracens—A large, upright growing shrub, with glossy, yellowish green leaves. A very effective lawn shrub. Pot-grown, one foot, 20c each; $1.50 per 10.

Polygala Damatiana—A profuse flowering shrub, with purple pea-blossom shaped flowers, and pretty light green foliage. Pot grown, one foot, 25c each.

Rhododendrons—These are among the grandest of our hardy flowering shrubs, and cannot be surpassed for lawn decoration. The flowers range through shades of rose, pink, crimson, white, etc. We have a magnificent collection of strong, vigorous plants. Should be planted in partial shade. Price, $1.50 each

Swainsona galegifolia alba—This variety has delicate white flowers. 25c each.

Araucaria Imbricata · Photographed by Cox Seed Co.

Swainsona Greyana—(*Darling River Pea*)— Flowers rose color, produced in sprays of from twelve to twenty flowers each, the individual blooms resembling the flowers of a sweet pea. Leaves small, acacia-like. 25c each.

Sciadopytis verticillata—Commonly called "Umbrella Pine." Two to three feet. $1.50 each.

Thujopsis dolobrata—Leaves shining green above, silvery white beneath. Of a pendulous and dwarfish habit. Branchlets coral-like in appearance. A most peculiar looking tree; from Japan. One foot, 50c each.

Veronica imperialis—The finest of the species. Flowers amaranth. Two feet, 35c each.

Veronica Variegated—A handsome shrub, with blue flowers and variegated foliage. Two feet, 35c each.

Yew, Irish—Deep blackish green foliage. Of erect growth. Much used in cemetery work. Four feet, $1.50 each

Deciduous Trees and Shrubs

Hawthorne   Photographed by Cox Seed Co.

Almond, Large Double Flowering — (*Double White, Pink and Crimson*). Four to five feet, 50c each.

Ash, European—A lofty tree of rapid growth, with spreading head and gray bark. Pinnate leaves and black buds. Six to eight feet 50c each.

Beech, European—A beautiful tree attaining a height of sixty to eighty feet. Two feet, 50c each.

Beech, Purple-Leaved—Foliage is deep purple in spring, changing to crimson in the fall. Two to three feet, $1 50 each.

Berberry, Purple-Leaved — The foliage of this shrub is very beautiful, being of a dark reddish purple. Three to four feet, 40c each.

Birch, European White—Remarkable for its elegance. Very graceful, with silvery bark and slender branches. Six to eight feet, 75c each.

Calycanthus floridus—(*Sweet Shrub*) — A very desirable shrub, with fragrant wood and rich foliage. Flowers a rare chocolate color, having a peculiar, agreeable odor. 35c each.

¶**Catalpa Kæmpferii**—A rapid growing, spreading, irregular tree, with large heart-shaped leaves. Remarkable for its clusters of white fragrant flowers, in spring. Six to eight feet, 60c each.

Cherry, Japanese, Double Flowering –A very ornamental shrub (or small tree), producing immense masses of large double pink and double white flowers. 50c each.

Chionanthus Virginicus — A small growing tree, of roundish form, with large glossy leaves and drooping racemes of pure white flowers. A superb lawn tree. Two feet, 50c each.

Corchorus Japonicus—Produces globular-shaped, deep yellow flowers for a long period. Foliage slender and graceful. Three feet, 50c each.

Deutzia crenata—The deutzias are among the showiest of our shrubs, producing their flowers all along the branches in the spring-time. This variety has white flowers, suffused pink. Two to three feet, 30c each.

Deutzia gracilis—This variety is dwarf-growing and produces its pure white flowers in prodigal luxuriance. One and a half feet, 40c each.

Deutzia Scabra—Flowers bell-shaped, coming in small bunches. Foliage oval. Very rough underneath. Two to three feet, 30c each.

Dogwood, Red Twigged—Very striking in winter, when the blood-red branches are seen to advantage. Three feet, 30c each.

Elm, American, White - A magnificent large tree, with drooping, spreading branches. Six feet, 50c each.

Elm, Corkbark—A valuable shade-tree, and very desirable for streets and avenues. Young branches very corky. Leaves rough on both sides. Eight to ten feet, 75c

Forsythia viridissima (*Golden Bell*)— Very showy shrubs, producing their yellow flowers in early spring before the appearance of the leaves. Two to three feet, 30c each.

Honeysuckle, Tartarian (*Upright or Bush*)—This variety of honeysuckle is a bush sort, excellent for the formation of hedges. Beautiful creamy-white flowers. Two feet, 30c each.

Hydrangea paniculata grandiflora — A very striking and elegant hardy flowering shrub, suitable for lawns. The flowers are pure white. 35c each.

Hypericum patulum—(St. John's Wort)—A most desirable shrub; it has single flowers of buttercup yellow. 25c each.

Hypericum Moserianum—A new variety similar to the preceding, but produces its beautiful flowers more freely. 35c each.

Laburnum or Golden Chain—A beautiful small garden tree, with long drooping racemes of fragrant yellow flowers. 50c each.

Lemon Verbena—The fragrance from the foliage of this old favorite is delightfully refreshing. 40c each.

Lilac—Purple, White and Red. 40c each.

Linden, American—A rapid growing, large sized tree with very large leaves and fragrant flowers. 60c each.

Locust, Bessoniana (*Thornless*)—The most ornamental of all the locust family. Forms a solid, compact head, with dark green, luxuriant foliage. Eight to ten feet, 75c.

DECIDUOUS TREES AND SHRUBS—Continued.

Snowball   Photographed by Cox Seed Co.

Locust. Common or Black—A rapid-growing tree with spreading branches. A valuable lumber tree, and used for various mechanical purposes. Eight to ten feet. 60c each.

Locust. Decnaisneana (*Pink Flowering*) – Remarkable for its vigorous growth and its fine rose-colored flowers. · Eight to ten feet, 75c each.

Locust Hispida (*Robinia hispida*)—Rose or Moss Locust. This variety is of irregular growth, and is chiefly prized for the beautiful deep rose-colored flowers which it produces very freely during June and July. Two to three feet, 50c each.

Maiden Hair Tree (*Salisburia*)—A beautiful tree from Japan. The leaves are shaped like those of the Maiden Hair Fern, only larger. Very choice. Two feet, 50c each.

Magnolia, Japanese Flowering — Good assortment. Three feet, 50c each.

Maple, Japanese—None of our autumnal trees can excel these in gorgeousness of coloring they include yellow, blood-red, green and variegated. The uniqeness of the shape of the leaves is also wonderful, some as delicate as the finest lace. Plant in shady place. One to two feet, 60c each.

Mock Orange (*Philadelphus*)—A vigorous class of shrub, with large handsome foliage and beautiful milk white flowers produced in the greatest profusion, early in the summer.

Mock Orange (*Coronarius*)—Flowers pure white, delightful. orange-blossom fragrance. Three to four feet 40c each.

Mock Orange (*Grandiflorus*) — A tall bush, of slender, twiggy habit, with large flowers, slightly fragrant. Three to four feet, 40c each; four to six feet, 60c each.

Mock Orange—(*Gordonarius*)—Three to four feet, 30c each.

Mountain Ash, European (*Rowan Tree*)—Flowers creamy white. Foliage somewhat like the Pepper Tree. Covered from August to November with large clusters of orange-colored berries. Six to eight feet, 60c each.

Plum, Purple-leaved (*Pissardi*)—The young branches are a very dark purple. The leaves when young are lustrous crimson, changing to a dark purple, and retain this beautiful tint till they drop late in autumn. No other purple-leaved tree or shrub retains its color like this. It also bears a fairly good fruit. Three to four feet, 50c each.

Purple Fringe, Mist Tree, Smoke Tree (*Rhus continus*)—Variously known by these names. It is much admired. It produces curious fringe or hair-like flowers that cover the plant in summer time. Three feet, 40c each.

Quince Scarlet Flowering—These are among the first flowers to herald spring in. They are scarlet, and produced along the branches before the appearance of the leaves, and are greatly admired. One and a half feet, 30c each.

Snowball—Produces large, globular, pure white flowers in great luxuriance. Three to four feet, 50c each.

Spiræa—We consider these shrubs among the prettiest, and can fully recommend them. When spring is at its brightest, the spiræs are among the showiest of flowering shrubs.

Spiræa callosa—The flowers are produced in large panicles of a deep rosy hue. Three feet, 30c each.

Spiræa pruniflora (*Bridal Wreath*)—This is probably the favorite. Flowers double, small, produced among the branches. Three to four feet, each 40c

Spiræ Van Houttii— White flowers. Three to four feet, 40c each.

Mock Orange.   Photographed by Cox Seed Co.

DECIDUOUS TREES AND SHRUBS—Continued.

Tamarix Africana—The foliage of this shrub is most graceful and feathery. The flowers are spike-shaped, and of a pinkish hue. Three to four feet, 35c each.

Tamarix Gallica—Three to four feet, 35c each.

Texas Umbrella—(*Melia Azedarach Umbraculiformis*—Entirely different from the Pride of China. Takes the shape of an umbrella is of striking beauty, and one of the handsomest of shade-trees. Five to six feet, 50c each; six to eight feet, 80c each.

Thorn, Double Pink—Three to four feet, 35c; six feet, 60c.

Thorn, Double White—Has small double white flowers. A highly ornamental variety, on account of both foliage and flowers. Three to four feet. 35c each.

Thorn, Paul's Double Scarlet—Three to four feet, 35c each.

Thorn, Single Pink—Three to four feet, 35c each.

Weigilea rosea—Elegant shrub from Japan. They produce superb, large, trumpet-shaped flowers of a fine rose color. Two to three feet, 35c each.

Willow, Common (*Babylonica*) — The well-known weeping willow. 35c each.

Climbing and Trailing Plants.

Ampelopsis Veitchii.   Photographed by Cox Seed Co.

Akebia quinata—A very distinct and pretty climber from Japan. Foliage clover-like in appearance, semi-evergreen. Flowers chocolate colored, appearing in early spring. very sweet. 50c each.

Ampelopsis quinquefolia (*Virginia Creeper*)—Leaves palmate, handsome and luxuriant, assuming in autumn a gorgeous bronzy hue. Small plants, 25c each; strong, 35c each.

Ampelopsis Veitchii (*Boston or Japan Ivy*)—A great improvement on the old Virginia Creeper. Fast growing in the shade or sun. 25c and 35c each.

Asparagus Plumosus Nanus—The leaves are a bright green, are gracefully arched and are as finely woven as the finest silk mesh, surpassing Maiden-Hair Ferns in grace, fineness of texture and richness of color. 35c and 50c each.

Asparagus Sprengerii—A variety of recent introduction. It is as a basket plant that this will prove most valuable. 10c, 25c and 50c each.

Asparagus tennuissimus—Is a very pleasing house plant. Its graceful branches are freely produced, and take the place of smilax. 25c; large plants 50c each. (THE ASPARAGUS ARE FOR INSIDE CULTURE ONLY.)

Australian Pea Vine – Pink flowers. Fast growing. 25c each.

Bignonia grandiflora (*Trumpet Vine*) — Rapid growing climber. bearing large orange yellow trumpet-shaped flowers in great profusion. 50c each.

Bignonia radicans—Flowers scarlet. Very free in growth and bloom. 35c each.

Clematis Jackmani — Deep violet purple flowers, produced in masses; single, $1.00 each.

CLIMBING AND TRAILING PLANTS—Continued.

Ficus (Rubber Tree)

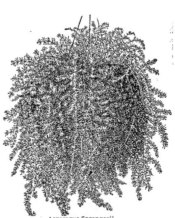

Asparagus Sprengerii

Clianthus—(*Scarlet Parrot's Bill*)—Fast growing. Very bright. Small Plants, 15c each.

Honeysuckle, English—Flowers very fragrant. Produced for a long period. Strong plants, 35c each.

Honeysuckle, Gold Netted—A beautiful variety. The leaves are veined golden yellow. Small plants, 15c each; large plants, 25c each.

Honeysuckle, Halleana, Hall's Japan Honeysuckle—A strong, vigorous, almost evergreen sort, with pure white flowers, changing to yellow. Very fragrant. A long and continuous bloomer 25c each.

Honeysuckle, Yellow—A well-known variety. Yellow trumpet-shaped flowers. 25c each.

Ivy, English, Large Leaved—Leaves thick, shining, leathery 35c each.

Ivy, English, Small-leaved—Small plants, 15c each; large plants, 35c each.

Ivy, Variegated, Silver-leaved—Small plants, 15c each; large plants, 35c each.

Jasmine Nudiflorum (*Yellow Flowering Jasmine*)—Produces fragrant yellow flowers. 25c each.

Madeira Vine—A very handsome vine, of rapid growth, bearing numerous white flowers. 5c; 6 for 25c.

Plumbago Capensis—Can be trained as a bush or climber. Flowers light sky-blue, verbena-shaped, produced throughout the entire summer. Stands drought and water and the brightest sunshine. 25c each.

Passion Vine, Blue—25c each.

Passion Vine, Pink—35c each.

Passion Vine, Scarlet—35c each.

Passion Vine (*Constance Elliott*) **White**—25c each.

Muhlembeckia Complexa — This pretty, strong-growing climber and trailer is very desirable for covering old stumps of trees rock work, etc. The foliage is small, dense and graceful. 15c and 25c each.

Smilax—20c each; three for 50c.

Wistaria Sinensis—This is one of our most admired climbers, blooming in early spring. The flowers appear in long grape-like clusters of a beautiful lavender color. Price $1.00 each.

Wistaria Sinensis Alba—A fine variety with pure white flowers. Price $1.00.

Withania Organifolia, Climbing Lily of the Valley—25c each.

Palms, Dracænas, Etc.

Areca Sapida—75c each.

Brahea edulis—A new variety of Fan Palm, from Guadaloupe Island. The best Fan Palm for out-doors. 60c, $1.00 and $4.00 each.

Brahea filamentosa—(*Prichardia filamentosa—Washingtonia filefera*)—The hardy California Fan Palm, a hardy, vigorous growing plant. 35c, 60c and $1.50 each.

Corypha Australis (*Livistonia*)—A very ornamental Australian Palm; foliage dark green; very symmetrically and regularly slit, the segments partly doubled from base of petioles or leaf stalk, which is thickly armed with crooked spines. 50c, $1.00 and $1.50 each.

Chamærops humilis—A Fan Palm of dwarf habit. It is a native of Southern Europe; very hardy. A splendid specimen for the lawn. 75c each.

Chamærops excelsa—One of the hardiest of the Fan Palms; foliage dark green; the segments of the fan-shaped leaves deeply cut, the edges covered with tooth-like spines; grows from 15 to 20 feet high; very desirable for out-door decorating. 50c and $1.00 each.

Chamærops Nepaulensis—$1.50 each.

Cycas Revoluta—(*Sago Palm*)—50c, 75c, $1.00, $2.00, $2.50 each.

Dracæna Indivisa—A fine plant for out-door planting in California, and much in use for lawns, avenues and parks. The small plants are fine for window decorations. 50c, 75c and $1.00 each.

Kentia Belmoreana—This fine Palm is a valuable addition to our collections; its leaves are pinnate, dark green, and so beautifully crisp as to gain for it the name of the "Curly Palm." It is very elegant and graceful in habit. 20c, 35c and $1.00 each.

PALMS, DRACÆNAS, ETC.—Continued.

Kentia Canterburyana—An excellent decorative variety. 50c each.

Kentia Fosteriana—One of the finest of the Kentias, with graceful bright green foliage. 35c and $1.00 each.

Latania Borbonica—Leaves large, fan-shaped, of a very cheerful green color; plant of a hardy constitution, and adapted to all decorative purposes within doors. 15c, 75c and $1.50 each.

Musa Ensete (Abyssinian Banana)—50c

Phœnix Canariensis—The hardiest and handsomest species of the Date Palm family. Being a rapid grower, it soon develops into beautiful specimens, with pinnate, dark green leaves from 6 to 12 feet long. the divisions linear, lance-shaped, very much pointed. 25c, 50c, $1.00, $1.50, $2.50 and $3.00

Phœnix farinifera—50c each.

Phœnix paludosa—50c each.

Phœnix pumillea—50c each.

Phœnix rupicola—50c each.

Raphis flabelliformis—A hardy little Cane Palm, which succers from the roots like the bamboo, and forms a dense clump of canes. A delicate and graceful little plant, only 3 to 4 feet in height when full grown. 75c each.

Indoor Decorative Plants.

Australian Tree Fern.

Under this heading we have included such plants and ferns as flourish in the parlor, hall, conservatory, and some in protected situations out of doors.

Australian Tree Fern—$2.50, $5.00, $7.50 and $10.00 each.

Asplenium falcatum—25c and $1.00 each.

Adiantum cuneatum—(*Maiden Hair Fern*)—40c, 60c, 75c and $1.00 each.

Aralia Sieboldii—Leaves fig leaf in shape. 35c and 75c each.

Begonias—In good assortments. 25c each.

Carex Japonica Variegata—Very useful for hanging baskets. 25c each.

Coleus—We have a grand lot of these ever popular plants. 25c and 35c each.

Isolepsis gracilis—A pretty grass-like plant, valuable for hanging baskets. 20c each.

Nephrolepsis exaltata (*Sword Fern*)—25c; 50c and 75c each.

Nephrolepsis exaltata Bostoniensis—(*Boston Sword Fern*)—35c and 50c each.

Pandanus Utilis—(*Screw Pine*)—35c each.

Rubber Tree—Large plants $1.50 each; smaller, 75c.

Umbrella Plant—35c and 50c each.

Miscellaneous Plants.

Abutilon—White, Yellow, Souvenir de Bonn, Pink. 25c each.

Auricula—15c each.

Cannas—In best assortment. 25c each.

Dahlias—Including the following select varieties: American Flag, Apple Blossom, Hohenzollern, Loreley, Island Queen, Countess of Pembroke, Mrs. Munro, Gloriosa, Kaiser William, Maid of Kent, Miss May Loomis, Matchless, Mrs. Hartong. 25c each. For full list see our annual catalogue.

Daisy—35c per doz.

Echeveria (*Hen and Chickens*)—50c per doz.

FUCHIAS

Strong plants, 25c each.

E. G. Hill—Best double white; very large.

Phenomenal—Best double purple; very large.

Storm King—Double white, suffused pink.

Gazania Splendens—10c each; 75 per doz.

GERANIUMS

15c each; $1.50 per doz., comprising the best varieties in Common, Ivy-Leaved, Nutmeg, Peppermint, Rose-Leaved and Silver-Leaved.

HELIOTROPES

Strong Plants, 20c each.

Picola—Rosy violet.

Queen—Very dark.

Sapphire—Purple, white center.

Snow-wreath—White.

Hydrangea Hortensis—25c each.

Libonia Florabunda—10c each.

Marguerite, White, Yellow and Blue—15c each.

Pansies—Our pansies are unequaled for size, form and color. 50c a doz.; $3.00 per 100

Sea Pink—50c a doz.

MISCELLANEOUS PLANTS—Continued.

Beauty of Glazenwood Rose.

Photographed by Cox Seed Co.

Spergula—Used in place of grass; requires no cutting, 50c per square foot.

Sunflower, Single Perennial — 10c each, 3 for 25c.

VIOLETS

These are one of our Specialties, Growing Them in Large Quantities. 50c per dozen; $3.00 per 100.

Imperial (*New*)—Grand; single; deep violet blue.

Luxonne (*New*)—Best double blue.

Princess of Wales—Beautiful violet blue in color, sweetly fragrant and flowering continually from September until April.

The California — Color clear violet purple; fragrance intense; flowers borne on long stems 10 to 14 inches in length.

Single White.

ROSES

Strong field grown, 25c each, $2.50 per dozen; extra sized plants 35c each, $3.50 per dozen; ready for shipment December 1st.

Following we give an abbreviated list:

American Beauty—Glowing deep carmine.

Anna de Diesbach—Brilliant crimson.

Augustine Guinnosseau—White La France.

Banksia, White and Yellow—Climbers.

Beauty of Glazenwood— Coppery yellow Climber

Belle Siebrecht—Silvery rose color.

Black Prince—Very dark.

Bride—Superb White.

Bridesmaid—Unexcelled pink.

Captain Christy—Beautiful flesh color.

Caroline Testout--Bright pink.

Catherine Mermet—Lovely pink.

Cherokee, Double and Single — White climbers.

Chestnut Hybrid--Cherry-carmine; climber.

Claire Carnot—Coppery rose, shaded amber; climber.

Climbing Devoniensis—Good White.

Climbing Perle des Jardins—Fine yellow.

Comptesse de Frigneuse—Deep yellow.

Climbing La France—Pink.

Crimson Rambler—Bright crimson; climber.

Doctor Grill--Buff pink.

Duchesse de Brabrant—Rosy blush.

Duchess of Albany—Rosy pink.

Duchess of Edinburgh—Deep crimson.

Emperor of Morocco—Very dark.

MISCELLANEOUS PLANTS—Continued.

ROSES—Cont'd.

General Jaqueminot—Glowing scarlet.
Glorie de Margottin — Intense deep scarlet; climber,
Gold of Ophir—Salmon yellow.
Grace Darling—Beautiful blending of pink and white.
Isabella Sprunt--Canary yellow.
Kaiserina Augusta Victoria—Extra good white.
La Marque--Pure white; climber.
Madame Hoste—Yellowish white.
Madam de Watteville—Beautifully blended.
Manda's Triumph—Creeping rose.
Marechal Niel—Deep yellow; climber.
Mrs. John Laing—Beautiful pink.
Niphetos--Pure White.
Papa Gontier--Rich crimson.
Perle des Jardins—Straw yellow
Perle d'Or--"Baby Rose," nankeen yellow,
Rainbow Improved — Pink, blotched and striped.
Reine Marie Henriette—Crimson; climber.
Reine Olga de Wurtemburg—Rosy crimson; climber.
Reeve d'Or—Deep yellow; climber.
Safrano—Apricot-yellow.

Shirley Hibberd—Nankeen yellow.
Sunset—Rich deep yellow.
Sweet Briars—Assorted.
Ulrich Bruner—Cerise red.
William Allen Richardson—Orange-yellow.
White Maman Cochet—Extra fine white.

CARNATIONS.

For the present we can offer strong plants, grown in 4-inch pots. of the following varieties, at 25c each, $2.50 per dozen. (We refer our customers to general Annual Catalogue issued January 1st, for a larger and more comprehensive list.)
Edward Schwerin—A superb pink.
Ethel Crocker—An ideal shade of pink.
Flora Hill—Best white.
General Gomez—Cardinal Maroon.
Iris Miller—Salmon, shaded yellow.
Jonathan Bourn,Jr—Glossy lavender, blotched and striped bright carmine. A most odd and beautiful sort.
Mrs. Thomas Lawson—Beautiful deep pink.
Pansy Kelly—Yellow, beautifully striped pink.
President Roosevelt—Best dark.
Prosperity—White, mottled pink. Very large; beautiful as an azalea.
Sally McKee- Cherry red; superb.

Fruit Trees and Small Fruits
ORDERS BOOKED NOW. WRITE FOR PRICES ON LARGE LOTS.

APPLES

Price, four to six feet, 30c each; $2.50 per 10.
Alexander—Very large and showy; yellow streaked with red. Ripe in September and October.
Baldwin—Large, roundish; deep bright red over a yellow ground. Ripe in November and December.
Lawver—Very large; brilliant red, covered with small dots. Ripe December to April.
Red Astrachan—Large, roundish; skin deep red; flesh white. Ripe in June and July.
White Winter Pearmain—Large, roundish oblong and pale yellow, dotted with brown. Ripe December to February.
Yellow Bellflower—Very long; oblong, irregular and tapering towards the eye; skin smooth and of pale yellow color. Ripe November to February.
Yellow Newton Pippin—Large; flesh yellow, firm, crisp, juicy, of exceedingly rich flavor. Ripe January to March.

CRAB APPLES

Price same as Apples.
Red Siberian—Fruit about an inch in diameter; yellow, with a scarlet cheek.
Yellow Siberian (*Golden Beauty*)—Large; color beautiful golden yellow.

PEARS

[Price, four to six feet, 30c each; $2.50 per 10.]
Bartlett—There is no occasion to describe this variety, so well known is it. Ripe in August.
Beurre Clairgeau—Very large; red cheek with russet ground; bears very heavily and when quite young; flesh rather coarse at the core. Ripe in October.

Beurre Diel--Large. roundish; productive; color lemon yellow, with russet dots; delicious, buttery flavor. Ripe in October.
Beurre Hardy—Large, brown, smooth; very fine flavor; buttery and delicious. Ripe in September.
Seckel—Quite small; rich, yellowish brown; very sweet and productive. Ripe in September.
P. Barry—The color of fruit is deep yellow, nearly covered with rich golden russet; very large. Best of all late pears Ripe January to March.
Winter Nelis—Medium size; roundish; yellowish green, dotted with russet; fine flavor. Ripe November to January.

CHERRIES.

Price, four to five feet, 30c each; $2.50 per 10.
Black Tartarian—Very large; bright black. The favorite.
Gov. Wood—Light yellow, blotched red. Early.
Napoleon Bigarreau (*Royal Ann*)—Very large; amber in color. The favorite white cherry.
Rockport Bigarreau—Large, bright red.
May Duke—Large, dark red; fine. This is one of the sorts used for making pies.
Reine Hortense—Very large; red. Another of the sour sort.

PLUMS

Price, four to six feet, 30c each; $2.50 per 10
Burbank—Large, yellowish ground, with red cheek; flesh yellow, firm and very sweet when fully ripe.
Coe's Golden Drop—Large, oval; yellow.
California Red Plum—Extra large; deep blue, with reddish cast on cheek; clings tight to the tree; flesh very firm, and one of the best shipping plums. Ripens in July.

Clyman—Large, reddish purple; flesh firm; freestone. Very vigorous and a heavy bearer. The best of early plums.

Duane's Purple—Of grand size and handsome; reddish purple; lilac bloom; flesh juicy, moderately sweet and mild flavor; adheres to the stone.

Jefferson—A fine variety; large oval, yellow, with reddish cheek; flesh very rich juicy, and of high flavor; freestone.

Royal Hative—Medium size; roundish; skin light purple, flesh yellow, amber; rich and high flavored.

Yellow Egg—Very large and beautiful egg-shaped plum; flesh yellow, rather acid until fully ripe when it sweetens; clingstone.

PRUNES

Price, Prune on Myrobolan, four to six feet, 30c each, $2 50 per 10

French Prune—This is the Prune now grown so extensively and successfully for drying purposes.

Hungarian—Fruit very large with tendency to come double; reddish violet; covered with a handsome bloom; very juicy and sweet.

Imperial Epineuse (*New*)—Large and uniform in size; very sweet and of high flavor; the skin is thin, and of a reddish purple when green; when dried coal black.

Robe de Sargent—Medium size; oval; skin deep purple, approaching black, and covered with thick blue bloom; flesh greenish yellow, sugary; rich and luscious.

Silver—Very large; oval; skin yellow. Makes a very attractive dried fruit, besides being a good shipper and canner.

Tragedy—This is the earliest of all Prunes, and earlier than any Plum. Good size; dark purple skin; yellowish green flesh; sweet and very rich.

A NEW PRUNE—"SUGAR"

Price, three to four feet, 30c each; $2 50 per 10

NECTARINES

Price, four to six feet, 30c each; $2 50 per 10

Early Newington—One of the very earliest.

Lord Napier—Large; pale cream color with dark red cheek; flesh white, melting, tender and juicy

New white—Large; skin white; flesh white, tender and very juicy; of rich vinous flavor.

QUINCES

Price, four to five feet, 35c each; $3 00 per 10

Apple or Orange—Large; bright yellow; the best.

Champion—Very large; flavor delicate, imparting an exquisite quince taste and odor to any fruit with which it is cooked.

Portugal—Very large; turns a fine purple or deep crimson when cooked.

APRICOTS

Price, three to five feet; 30c each; $2 50 per 10

Hemskirke—A large and very fine Apricot.

Moorpark—Largest size; rich yellow.

Royal—A fine early variety; popular in many places as a regular bearer.

Shipley (*Blenheim*)—Above medium; flesh juicy, rich.

PEACHES

Price, 1 year, four to five feet. 30c. each; $2 50 per 10

Alexander—Most widely grown being considered the best early variety; medium to large; greenish white, nearly covered with deep red; flesh firm, juicy and sweet.

Early Crawford—This is probably the most extensively grown of all peaches.

Foster—Large, yellow, very rich and juicy.

Lovell—Yellow freestone; uniformly large; superior for canning and shipping.

Muir—The best of all peaches for drying, because it loses less than any other in the process. Has a delicious, rich, buttery, sweet flavor.

Nichols' Orange Cling—Large; yellow, with purple cheek; flesh yellow and good.

Newhall—Very large; skin yellow, with dark red cheek; flesh deep yellow; juicy, and of rich vinous flavor.

Phillips' Cling—Fine large yellow Cling, showing no color at pit. which is very small.

Salway—A large yellow. English peach, with deep yellow flesh; very juicy, melting and rich. The most valuable late market variety.

FIGS

Price, three to four feet, 35c each; $3 00 per 10

California black—A well-known local variety; large dark purple, almost black when fully ripe.

White Adriatic—Tree a strong and healthy grower; fruit above medium size; skin white and thin; pulp red, fine, exceedingly aromatic, and changes to an amber color when dried.

GRAPES—Foreign Varieties.

Price, 15c each; $1 00 per 10

Black Hamburg—Bunches and berries large: black, very sugary and rich.

Black Morocco—Very large; rich and sweet.

Black Ferrera—One of the latest and most firm grapes known.

California Black—The well-known Mission grape.

Cornichon—Berries very large; oblong; covered with beautiful bloom; skin rather thick and dark.

Emperor—Bunches large, with large oval, rose-colored berries.

Flame Tokay—A magnificent large, red grape.

Muscat Hamburg—A new variety; resembles Black Hamburg.

Muscat of Alexandria—Bunches and berries large, pale amber.

Purple Damascus—A large, fine, oval grape, of fine quality.

Rose of Peru—Very large bunches; berries rounding, brownish black.

Sweetwater—Bunches good size; berries medium size, round fruit.

Zante—The grape from which the currant of commerce is made.

Assorted Small Fruits

Grapes, American, assorted, 20c each; $1 50 per 10
Currants, assorted, 15c each; $1 00 per 10
Gooseberry, " 15c each, $1 00, per 10
Blackberries, assorted 10c each; 75c per 10
Raspberry, Red. 10c each; 75c per 10
    " Yellow & Black. 15c each, $1 00 per 10
Strawberries, assorted, 25c per 12; $1 50 per 100
Loganberries, 15c each; $1 00 per 10

Cox Seed Company

411=415 SANSOME ST.
SAN FRANCISCO
CALIFORNIA

Photographed by Cox Seed Co.

PHŒNIX CANARIENSIS ✐ Canary Island Date Palm

NURSERIES:
Glen Avenue, near Mountain View Cemetery,
OAKLAND, CAL.

CPSIA information can be obtained
at www.ICGtesting.com
Printed in the USA
BVHW051453261118
534009BV00035B/3432/P

9 781528 118934